W9-DAZ-812

DOS

THE POCKET REFERENCE

Kris Jamsa

Osborne **McGraw-Hill**
Berkeley, California

Osborne **McGraw-Hill**
2600 Tenth Street
Berkeley, California 94710
U.S.A.

For information on translations and book distributors outside of the
U.S.A., please write to Osborne **McGraw-Hill** at the above address.

IBM is a trademark of IBM Corp.

DOS: The Pocket Reference

234567890 DODO 898

ISBN 0-07-881376-x

Editor: Kay Luthin
Word Processor: Bonnie Bozorg
Production: Kevin Shafer

CONTENTS

INTRODUCTION

This pocket reference is a convenient guide for both novice and experienced DOS users. It contains information on every DOS command, including complete examples and a discussion of each of the DOS system configuration parameters.

If you have already worked with DOS, you are aware of its tremendous functionality. You are also aware that no user could possibly remember each of the many DOS commands and their options. You will find that this pocket reference is an invaluable tool—successful DOS users have well-worn pocket reference guides.

For more detailed information about DOS, refer to *DOS: The Complete Reference,* by Kris Jamsa (Osborne/McGraw-Hill, 1987) or *DOS Power User's Guide,* by Kris Jamsa (Osborne/McGraw-Hill, 1988).

DOS SYSTEM CONFIGURATION

Each time DOS boots, the DOS startup procedures search the root directory on the boot drive for the CONFIG.SYS file. If DOS finds this file, it opens and reads it, using its contents to configure the operating system in memory. If DOS does not find this file, it uses its default values to configure the operating system.

The CONFIG.SYS file contains entries that DOS uses to define specific operating system attributes. Be careful when you place entries into CONFIG.SYS; each entry directly affects a specific portion of the operating system. Incorrect entries, therefore, can degrade your system's performance significantly. As a rule, make a copy of your existing CONFIG.SYS file before you modify its contents.

Once you modify an entry in CONFIG.SYS, you must reboot the operating system to make the change take effect.

The following sections describe each of the DOS system configuration entries.

BREAK

Increases the number of functions that DOS will examine (upon completing each function) for a user-entered CTRL-BREAK in the keyboard buffer. The default is BREAK=OFF.

The only way to terminate most "runaway" DOS applications is to press CTRL-C or CTRL-BREAK. By default, each time DOS sends output to a screen or printer or receives keyboard input, it checks to see if the user has pressed CTRL-BREAK. If the user has done so, DOS terminates the current application. By using the setting of BREAK=ON, you can increase the number of functions for which DOS will perform CTRL-BREAK checking. This also increases system overhead, since DOS must now spend considerable time simply testing for CTRL-BREAK. Most users, therefore, will leave the setting at BREAK=OFF.

Example

BREAK=ON   (Enables DOS extended
CTRL-BREAK checking)

BUFFERS

Defines the number of disk buffers that DOS places in memory to enhance disk input and output operations. The default is BUFFERS=3 (for disks greater than 360K).

Each time that DOS reads or writes information to disk, it transfers a sector (512 bytes) of information. If your program reads or writes records of data that are not exact multiples of 512 bytes, DOS simply buffers them in memory.

By increasing the number of buffers that DOS has available to it, you may be able to reduce the number of disk I/O operations that DOS must perform, and thereby speed operation time. However, if you increase the number too much, DOS will be hampered by system overhead, spending considerable time searching buffers.

Example

BUFFERS=25   (Good number for word
processing and database applications)

COUNTRY

Defines the country symbol set that DOS will support
for international considerations. The default is
COUNTRY=001.

Example

COUNTRY=001   (DOS Version 3.2 and earlier)

COUNTRY=001 437 C:\COUNTRY.SYS   (DOS
Version 3.3)

DEVICE

Allows you to install DOS device drivers at system
startup time.

  Each hardware device on your system—be it a
printer, disk drive, or screen display—requires
software that allows DOS to communicate with the
hardware. This software is called a device driver. For
devices that are standard to every computer system
(such as the screen, disk, keyboard, printer, and so on),
DOS provides device drivers within the operating sys-

tem itself. However, most third-party hardware devices, such as a plotter or a mouse, require their own device drivers. The DOS DEVICE CONFIG.SYS entry allows you to install the software required to inform DOS about the device.

Examples

DEVICE=ANSI.SYS   (Installs ANSI support)

DEVICE=VDISK.SYS 128 512 12   (Size=128K, 512-byte sectors, 12 directory entries)

FCBS

Allows you to specify the number of file-control blocks that will be concurrently opened by DOS. The default is FCBS = 4,0.

Prior to DOS Version 2.1, all DOS file operations were performed by means of file-control blocks (FCBs). If you are running older DOS applications, you may need to increase the number of FCBs that DOS supports.

Example

FCBS=12,4

FILES

Allows you to specify the maximum number of files that DOS can open simultaneously. The default is FILES=8.

By default, DOS provides storage for eight file handles. However, the first five are predefined, as shown here:

0   stdin (normally the keyboard)
1   stdout (normally the screen)
2   stderr (normally the screen)
3   stdaux (a serial communications device)
4   stdprn (the printer)

Keep in mind that because the first five file handles are predefined, DOS (by default) can only open three files simultaneously.

Example

    FILES=20

LASTDRIVE

Allows you to specify the drive letter of the last disk drive that DOS will support. The default is LAST-DRIVE=E.

Example

LASTDRIVE=I

SHELL

Allows you to specify the name and location of the DOS command processor that DOS is to use instead of the COMMAND.COM processor. The default for this setting is SHELL=COMMAND.COM.

Examples

SHELL=\DOS\COMMAND.COM   (DOS Version 3.2 and earlier)

STACKS

Allows you to define the default stack size.

Each time a hardware interrupt occurs on the IBM PC, DOS places the current machine state (registers) onto the hardware stack. If a large number of interrupts occur in succession, DOS may run out of stack space. In such cases, simply use the STACKS entry. The default depends on machine type.

Example

STACKS=8,32

DOS I/O REDIRECTION

Most DOS commands write their output to a predefined source called stdout (for standard output). By default, stdout points to your screen display. In a similar manner, DOS defines a standard input source for commands, called stdin. By default, stdin points to the keyboard. The DOS I/O redirection operators allow you to modify the source of input and the source of output for a command.

The DOS output redirection operator, > , allows you to direct the output of a command to a file or device in this manner:

    [C:\] DIR > FILENAME.EXT

In this example, rather than displaying the output to the screen, DOS will write the output to the file named FILENAME.EXT.

In a similar manner, the append redirection operator, >>, allows you to append the output of a command to a file. If the file specified does not exist, DOS creates it:

    [C:\] DIR >> OLDDIR.DAT

The DOS input redirection operator, < , allows you to modify a command's source of input from the keyboard to a file, as shown here:

```
[C:\] SORT < SOMEFILE.DAT
```

In this example, the DOS SORT command will obtain its input from the SOMEFILE.DAT file instead of the keyboard.

The DOS pipe operator, |, causes the output of one command to become the input of a second command:

```
[C:\] DIR | SORT
```

In this example, rather than displaying the result of the DIR command on the screen, DOS will route the output to the SORT command. As a result, a sorted directory listing will be displayed.

As you can see, DOS I/O redirection operators provide tremendous command-line flexibility.

COMMAND REFERENCE SECTION

This section takes a detailed look at each of the DOS commands. It presents each command's function and format, as well as notes on pertinent information and examples of the command's use. As you examine the commands, pay particular attention to the examples.

▶ APPEND

Function   Defines the data-file search path that DOS will use each time it fails to locate a file in the current directory or in a specified directory.

Format

> [*drive:*][*path*]APPEND [*d:*][*p*] [;[*d:*][*p*]...]

or

> [*drive:*][*path*]APPEND [/X][/E] (DOS Version 3.3)

where the following is true:

> *d:* specifies a disk drive that DOS is to include in the data search path.

> *p* specifies a DOS subdirectory to be included in the data-file search path.

> ... indicates that the disk drive and subdirectories can be specified several times.

> /X aids in SEARCH-FIRST, FIND-FIRST, and EXEC options. This is a DOS 3.3 qualifier.

> /E places an APPEND entry in the DOS environment in a manner similar to a PATH entry. Therefore, the DOS SET command can affect APPEND. This is a DOS 3.3 qualifier.

Notes   When DOS cannot find a data file as specified or in the current directory, it searches to see if the user has defined a data-file search path. The DOS APPEND command allows you to define disk drives and sub-directories to be included in this path.

Examples   In the following example, if DOS cannot find the data file in the current directory, it will search the root directories on drives C, B, and A, in that order:

    C> APPEND C:\;B:\;A:\

In a similar manner, the following APPEND command directs DOS to search \DOS, \UTIL, and then \MISC:

    C> APPEND \DOS;\UTIL;\MISC

▶ **ASSIGN**

Function   Routes disk-drive references from one disk drive to another.

Format

    ASSIGN [*source_drive* = *target_drive* [...]]

where the following is true:

source_drive is the disk-drive identifier of the disk from which I/O references should be routed.

target_drive is the disk-drive identifier of the disk to which I/O operations will be routed.

... indicates that the command can be repeated several times.

Notes Many older software packages look on drive A for data or overlay files. If you want to install such software on your fixed disk, you must trick the software into looking on the fixed disk for the files. ASSIGN allows you to do this.

If you invoke ASSIGN without any command-line parameters, ASSIGN will restore its original disk-drive assignments.

Do not place a colon after each disk-drive identifier in the ASSIGN command line.

Most users should consider using the DOS SUBST command instead of ASSIGN.

Examples In the following example, DOS disk I/O operations that reference drive A will be routed to the disk in drive C:

C> ASSIGN A=C

If you invoke a command such as

C> DIR A:

DOS will actually list the files contained on drive C.

The following command illustrates that you can perform multiple disk-drive assignments on one command line. In this case, DOS will route disk-drive requests from either drive A or drive B to drive C:

    C> ASSIGN A=C B=C

▶ ATTRIB

Function   Displays or modifies a file's attribute byte.

Format

    [*drive:*][*path*]ATTRIB [+A|-A] [+R|-R] *file_spec* [/S]

where the following is true:

+A directs ATTRIB to set a file's archive bit.

-A directs ATTRIB to clear a file's archive bit.

+R directs ATTRIB to set a file's read-only bit.

-R directs ATTRIB to clear a file's read-only bit.

file_spec is the complete DOS file specification, including the disk drive and path name, of the file or files to be modified. ATTRIB supports DOS wild-card characters.

/S directs DOS to process all files in the subdirectories below the specified directory. This is a DOS 3.3 qualifier.

Notes   Each DOS file has a directory entry, which contains an attribute byte. The DOS ATTRIB command modifies a file's attribute byte.

Several DOS commands, such as BACKUP, RESTORE, and XCOPY, use a file's attribute to enable selective file processing. By using these commands in conjunction with ATTRIB, you can gain considerable file-processing control.

Examples   If you do not specify the A or R qualifier, as shown here:

    [C:\] ATTRIB *.*

ATTRIB will display the current attributes of each file. In the command

    [C:\] ATTRIB +R CONFIG.SYS

ATTRIB will set the CONFIG.SYS file to read-only. This means that DOS cannot modify the file's contents. If you attempt to delete a read-only file, for example, DOS will display

    Access Denied

The DOS BACKUP /M qualifier directs BACKUP to back up only those files modified since the previous backup. By issuing the command

    [C:\] ATTRIB +A *.* /S

you can set the archive bit of every file on disk, thus in-
dicating that a backup is required for each. Similarly,
the command

    [C:\] ATTRIB -A *.* /S

marks each file as being backed up.

   ATTRIB can be used in conjunction with XCOPY
to copy the entire contents of a fixed disk to floppy
disks, still maintaining the original disk structure. First
mark all of the files on disk as requiring a backup:

    [C:\] ATTRIB +A *.* /S

Next, simply invoke XCOPY, as shown here:

    [C:\] XCOPY C:*.* A: /S /M

When the floppy disk fills, XCOPY will display a message stating so and then terminate. Insert a new floppy
disk in the drive and again repeat this process. XCOPY
will pick up with the first file marked as archived,
resuming the process at the correct location. Repeat this
process until XCOPY finds no files to copy.

▶ BACKUP

Function   Backs up one or more files to a new disk.

Format

[*drive:*] [*path*] BACKUP *source:* [*file_spec*] *target:*
[/A] [/D:*mm-dd-yy*] [/L:*log_file*] [/M] [/S]
[T:*hh:mm:ss*] [/F]

where the following is true:

source: specifies the source disk that contains the
file or files to be backed up.

file_spec is the DOS path name (or names) for the
file (or files) to back up.

target: specifies the target disk.

/A directs BACKUP to append source files to files
on the target disk.

/D:*mm-dd-yy* directs BACKUP to back-up files
modified since the specified date.

/L:*log_file* places an entry for all of the files in a
specified log file. BACKUP.LOG is the default.

/M directs BACKUP to back up files modified
since the last backup.

/S directs BACKUP to back up all subdirectory
files.

/T:*hh:mm:ss* directs BACKUP to back up files modified since the specified time. This is a DOS 3.3 qualifier.

/F tells DOS to format an unformatted disk. This is a DOS 3.3 qualifier.

Notes   BACKUP works closely with the system's directory entries to select specific files for backup. Note that DOS directory fields relate closely to BACKUP command-line qualifiers.

Examples   The following command backs up all of the files on drive C, including those in DOS subdirectories, to the floppy disk in drive A:

    [C:\] BACKUP C:*.* A: /S

The following command uses the BACKUP /A qualifier to add the C:TEST.DAT file to the files contained on the backup disk in drive B:

    [C:\] BACKUP C:TEST.DAT B: /A

Finally, this command directs BACKUP to back up only those files created since December 31, 1987:

    [C:\] BACKUP C:*.* A: /S /D:12:31:87

► BREAK

Function   Enables or disables DOS extended CTRL-BREAK checking.

Format

BREAK [ON | OFF]

where the following is true:

ON enables extended CTRL-BREAK checking.

OFF disables extended CTRL-BREAK checking.

Notes   By default, DOS checks for a user-entered CTRL-BREAK upon completing keyboard, screen, and printer I/O operations. If you enable extended CTRL-BREAK checking, DOS will also check for a user-entered CTRL-BREAK upon completing each system service, such as a disk read or write operation.

By enabling extended CTRL-BREAK processing, you increase the system overhead, since DOS must check for a CTRL-BREAK upon completing each system service. Therefore, programmers may want to set BREAK to ON during program development. Most users, however, will leave BREAK=OFF.

Examples   The following command enables DOS extended CTRL-BREAK checking:

C> BREAK ON

Invoking BREAK without including a command-line parameter causes it to display the current state of extended CTRL-BREAK checking:

C> BREAK
BREAK is on

▶ CALL

Function   Invokes a nested batch procedure from within a DOS batch file.

Format

CALL batch_file [argument[...]]

where the following is true:

batch_file is the name of the batch file containing the CALL nested procedure.

argument is the command-line parameter for the nested batch procedure.

Notes   DOS has difficulty invoking one batch file from within a second batch file when the invocation of the procedure appears in the middle of the batch file. If you must invoke a batch procedure in this manner, the CALL command enables you to do so.

This command functions similarly to the DOS COMMAND /C command within a batch file. This is a DOS 3.3 command.

Example As the following example shows, CALL can be included in a batch file to invoke a nested procedure:

```
CLS
CALL MYPROC
DATE
```

▶ **CHCP**

Function Displays or changes the current code page.

Format

CHCP [*code_ page*]

where the following is true:

code_ page specifies the desired code page. This parameter must have been previously prepared by the system as either the primary or secondary code page in CONFIG.SYS.

Notes CHCP is a DOS 3.3 command. Each time DOS displays a character on the screen, it must first map the ASCII value of the character to a specific letter in a character set. DOS uses code pages to map characters to letters.

DOS allows you to use different character sets for your DOS session, offering you international support. In order to select an alternate code page, you must have previously issued the NLSFUNC command.

Valid code-page entries include the following:

437	United States	863	French Canadian
850	Multilingual	865	Nordic
860	Portuguese		

If you invoke CHCP without a command-line parameter, CHCP will display the current code page.

Example   The following command directs CHCP to select the Nordic code page. Remember that this code page must have been prepared previously by an NLSFUNC command.

    [C:\] CHCP 865

▶ CHDIR

Function   Changes or displays the default directory.

Format

    CHDIR [*drive*:][*path*]

or

CD [*drive:*][*path*]

where the following is true:

drive: specifies the disk drive that contains the directory you want as the default. If you omit this parameter, CHDIR will use the current default.

path specifies the DOS path name for the current directory that you desire. If you omit the path, CHDIR will display the current directory.

Notes   CHDIR changes or displays the current directory name for the disk drive specified. Each time you specify a DOS path name for CHDIR, CHDIR will perform the following processing: If the path name is preceded with a slash, as in \SUBDIR, DOS will begin its search for the directory at the root. However, if the path name does not begin with a slash, as in SUBDIR, the subdirectory must reside below the current default directory.

DOS predefines two directory names, as shown here:

..   Parent directory of the current directory

.   Current default directory

Verify this by performing a directory listing of a DOS subdirectory, as shown here:

```
Volume in drive C is DOSDISK
Directory of C:\SUBDIR

.    <DIR> 11-01-87    11:34a
..   <DIR> 11-01-87    11:34a

     2 File(s)   7182336 bytes free
```

If you simply issue the following directory command:

```
[C:\] DIR .
```

DOS will display a directory listing for the current directory. However, if you instead use

```
[C:\] DIR ..
```

DOS will display the files in the parent directory.

Examples   Invoking CHDIR without a path name causes CHDIR to display the current directory:

```
[C:\] CD
C:\SUBDIR
```

This command is valid with a disk drive specifier, as shown here:

```
[C:\] CHDIR B:
B:\UTIL
```

In a similar manner, the following DOS CHDIR command selects the \DOS\CMDFILES subdirectory on drive B as the current default directory:

```
[C:\] CHDIR B:\DOS\CMDFILES
```

The user could actually issue this command as two separate commands, first selecting the subdirectory \DOS, like this:

```
[C:\] CD B:\DOS
```

and then selecting CMDFILES, like this:

```
[C:\] CD B:CMDFILES
```

Note the use of the leading backslash in the command

```
[C:\] CD B:\DOS
```

When the backslash is used, DOS looks for the subdirectory named DOS in the root directory of drive B. With the following command, however,

```
[C:\] CD B:CMDFILES
```

CHDIR will not look for the directory in the root, but rather in a subdirectory below the current directory (which is \DOS). If the command had been

   [C:\] CHDIR B:\CMDFILES

CHDIR would not have found the directory, since it would have looked in the root instead of in the current directory.

▶ CHKDSK

Function   Checks a disk's current status.

Format

   [*drive:*][*path*]CHKDSK [*d:*][*p*][*file_name*] [/F] [/V]

where the following is true:

   d: is the disk drive that CHKDSK is to examine.

   p specifies a DOS subdirectory that contains files that CHKDSK is to examine for disk fragmentation.

   file_name is the file name and extension of the file or files that CHKDSK is to examine for disk fragmentation.

   /F directs CHKDSK to fix errors found in a directory or FAT (file-allocation table).

/V directs CHKDSK to display the names of all files on the disk.

Notes   CHKDSK reports on the status of the following disk conditions:

- The amount of free, used, and corrupted disk space
- The number of hidden files
- The amount of free and used memory

Occasionally, as the normal day-to-day operation of a disk causes wear and tear on the storage media, files become corrupted and the files lose sectors. The DOS CHKDSK command allows you to view and even repair such discrepancies.

It is also possible for a DOS file to become fragmented, which means its contents are dispersed in different locations on the disk. The problem with fragmented files is that they increase system overhead on file I/O operations; the disk drive must rotate the disk several additional times in order to read the disk. The DOS CHKDSK command displays information on fragmented files as well. Once your disk becomes severely fragmented, you should consider a system backup-and-restore operation.

CHKDSK does not work with JOINed or SUBSTed disks.

By default, CHKDSK will only report disk errors—will not attempt to fix them. In order to write actual corrections to disk, use the /F qualifier.

Examples   The following command displays the state of the current disk:

   [C:\] CHKDSK

The output might be

   Volume DOSDISK created Oct 30, 1987 9:46pm

   21309440 bytes total disk space.
   0 bytes in 1 hidden files.
   208896 bytes in 91 directories.
   13871104 bytes in 1714 user files.
   20480 bytes in bad sectors.
   7206912 bytes available on disk.

   524288 bytes total memory
   401184 bytes free

If you specify a file specification or DOS wild-card characters, CHKDSK will report on disk fragmentation:

   [C:\] CHKDSK *.*

If fragmented files exist, CHKDSK will display

C:\FILENAME.EXT
contains n non-contiguous blocks.

If CHKDSK discovers errors while examining your disk contents, it will display

Volume DOSDISK created Oct 30, 1987 9:46pm

Errors found. F parameter not specified.
Corrections will not be written to disk.

1 lost clusters found in 1 chains.
Convert lost chains to files (Y/N)?
2048 bytes disk space would be freed.

To direct CHKDSK to repair the error, use the /F qualifier, as shown here:

[C:\] CHKDSK /F

Many users use CHKDSK to locate a file quickly. If you invoke CHKDSK with the /V qualifier, CHKDSK will display the name of every file on the disk:

[C:\] CHKDSK /V

► CLS

Function   Clears the screen display and places the cursor and DOS prompt in the home (upper-left) position.

Format

    CLS

Note   CLS does not affect video attributes.

Example   In the following example, DOS will erase the current screen contents, placing the cursor and the current DOS prompt in the home position:

    [C:\] CLS

► COMMAND

Function   Loads a secondary command processor.

Format

    COMMAND [drive:] [path] [/C string]
    [/E:num_bytes] [/P]

where the following is true:

drive: specifies the disk drive that contains the secondary command processor. If you do not specify this parameter, DOS will use the current default.

path is the DOS path name of the subdirectory that contains the command processor. If you do not specify a path name, DOS will use the current default.

/C *string* directs DOS to execute the command specified by *string*. This parameter is usually used for nested batch-file invocations.

/E:*num_bytes* specifies the size of the area that DOS is to allocate for the secondary command processor's environment space. This parameter must be between 160 and 32,767 bytes; the default is 160 bytes.

/P directs DOS to leave the secondary command processor permanently in memory.

Notes   Each time you load a secondary command processor, it obtains its own copy of the DOS environment space.

Most users use COMMAND to invoke nested batch procedures, as shown here:

```
CLS
COMMAND /C BATFILE
DATE
```

To terminate a secondary command processor, use the DOS EXIT command.

If you use the /P and /C parameters together, COMMAND will ignore /P.

Examples   In the following example, DOS will load the secondary command processor into memory only long enough to execute the CHKDSK command. Once the command terminates, DOS will remove the secondary command processor.

    [C:\] COMMAND /C CHKDSK

▶ **COMP**

Function   Displays the first ten differences between two files.

Format

    [drive:][path]COMP file_spec1 file_spec2

where the following is true:

   file_spec1 and *file_spec2* are the complete DOS path names of the files to be compared. COMP supports DOS wild-card characters.

Notes   COMP displays the differences between files as hexadecimal offsets into the file. If the files are identical, COMP will display the message

Files compare OK.

Upon completion of the file comparison, COMP will display

Compare more files (Y/N)?

To compare additional files, press Y; otherwise, you should press N.

If COMP locates more than ten differences, it will display

10 Mismatches - ending compare

COMP will not compare files of different sizes.

Examples In the following example, COMP will compare the contents of the file A.DAT to B.DAT:

[C:\] COMP A.DAT B.DAT

If you omit the file name from the secondary file, DOS will match the file name on the specified drive to the primary file:

[C:\] COMP A.DAT B:

If you do not specify a file in the COMP command line, COMP will prompt you for it.

► COPY

Function   Copies one or more files to the specified new destination.

Format

COPY *source_file* [/V][/A][/B] *target_file* [/V][/A][/B]

or

COPY *source1+source2* [/V][/A][/B][...] *target_file* [/V][/A][/B]

where the following is true:

source_file specifies the complete DOS file specification of the file to be copied.

/V tells COPY to use disk verification to ensure that a successful copy occurred. This qualifier adds processing overhead; however, it prevents a hardware error from rendering the contents of the source and target files inconsistent.

/A informs COPY that the preceding file was an ASCII file.

/B informs COPY that the preceding file was a binary file.

target_file is the name of the destination file. If a file matching the name of *target_file* exists, COPY will overwrite it.

source1+source2 indicates you can use any number of source files.

... indicates that several file names can reside on the command line.

Notes   COPY fully supports the use of DOS wild-card characters.

To combine multiple files into one file, use the plus sign (+) between the desired source files.

COPY will not allow you to copy a file to itself. If you attempt to do so, COPY will display

```
File cannot be copied onto itself
     0 file(s) copied.
```

Warning: COPY overwrites target files that have the same name.

Examples   The following command copies the contents of the CONFIG.SYS file to a file on drive B with the same name:

    [C:\] COPY A:CONFIG.SYS B:CONFIG.SYS

It is identical in function to the command

    [C:\] COPY A:CONFIG.SYS B:

or the commands

    [C:\] B:
    [B:\] COPY A:CONFIG.SYS

In the same manner, the command

    [C:\] COPY A:*.* B:*.*

copies all of the files on drive A to drive B. If you want to copy files contained in subdirectories below the current directory, use the XCOPY command.

    The following command uses the plus sign to append files B and C to file A, creating a file called D:

    [C:\] COPY A+B+C D

The following command allows you append text from the keyboard to an existing file, creating a new file:

    [C:\] COPY FILENAME+CON: NEWFILE.EXT

▶ **CTTY**

Function   Changes standard input/output to an auxiliary device.

Format

CTTY *device_name:*

where the following is true:

device_name: is the name of the desired device
for standard input.

Notes   Valid device names include AUX, COM1, and
COM2.

To return standard input to the console device, the
command CTTY CON must be issued through the
auxiliary device.

Example   The following command sets the standard
input/output to COM1:

CTTY COM1:

 DATE

Function   Sets the DOS system date.

Format

DATE [*mm-dd-yy*]

where the following is true:

mm is the desired month (1-12).

dd is the desired day (1-31).

yy is the desired year (80-99). DATE also allows you to include the century, in the form 19*yy*.

Notes The *mm-dd-yy* date format is dependent on the COUNTRY specifier in CONFIG.SYS. If you do not specify a date, DATE displays the current date.

Prior to DOS Version 3.3, the DATE command modified the AT system clock. Users of earlier versions must use the Setup disk provided with the *Guide to Operations* in order to change the AT system clock. DOS Version 3.3 TIME and DATE commands actually set this clock.

The actual date is an optional command-line parameter. If you omit the date, DATE will prompt you for it.

Examples In the following example, since the date was not present on the DOS command line, DATE prompted the user for it:

[C:\] DATE

The current date is: Sun 11-21-1987
Enter the new date: (mm-dd-yy)

If you simply want to display the system date without modifying it, press the ENTER key at the date prompt. DATE will leave the system date unchanged.

In the following example, DATE will set the system date to December 8, 1987:

    [C:\] DATE 12/08/87

This command is identical to

    [C:\] DATE 12/08/1987

As you can see, DATE fully supports a four-digit year.

Finally, this command illustrates how you can set the date from the DATE prompt:

    [C:\] DATE

    The current date is: Sun 11-01-1987
    Enter the new date: (mm-dd-yy) 12-08-87

▶ DEL

Function   Deletes a file from a disk.

Format

    DEL [*drive:*][*path*] *file_name* [*.ext*]

where the following is true:

file_name[*.ext*] is the name of the file to delete.
DEL fully supports DOS wild-card characters.

Notes   Unless overridden with a drive or path specifier, DEL will only delete files in the current directory.

DEL will not remove subdirectories. Use RMDIR for that purpose.

DOS allows you delete several specific files at one time by placing each file name on the command line.

If you attempt to delete all of the files in a directory, DOS will first prompt you with

Are you sure (Y/N)?

to ensure that you actually want the command performed. If you want to delete the files, press Y and press ENTER; otherwise, press N and press ENTER.

Warning: Once you have deleted a file, DOS cannot retrieve it.

Examples   In the following example, DEL will erase the contents of the CONFIG.OLD file from drive B:

[C:\] DEL B:CONFIG.OLD

In a similar manner, the command

[C:\] DEL \OS2\COMMANDS\STARTUP.BAK

will delete a file from within a DOS subdirectory.

If you attempt to delete all of the files in the current directory, like this:

[C:\] DEL *.*

DEL will respond with

Are you sure (Y/N)?

If you want to delete the files, press Y and press ENTER; otherwise, press N and press ENTER.

▶ **DIR**

Function   Displays a directory listing of files.

Format

DIR [*file_spec*] [/P] [/W]

where the following is true:

file_spec is the complete DOS file specification of the file or files for which DIR is to display the directory listing. It can contain a disk-drive identifier and path name. If you do not place a file specification in the command line, DIR will display a directory listing of all of the files in the current directory. DIR fully supports DOS wild-card characters.

/P directs DIR to pause after each screenful of information and display the prompt

Strike a key when ready. . .

/W directs DIR to display the files in short form (file name only), with five file names across the screen.

Notes   DIR will display the complete name, size in bytes, and the date and time of creation or last modification for each file. DIR also displays the amount of free disk space in bytes. It does not display hidden system files.

   To list all of the files on disk, including files in DOS subdirectories, use the TREE command.

   DIR always displays the drive and directory in which the files are stored, as shown here:

Volume in drive A is DOSDISK
Directory of A:\

SUBDIR   <DIR>   11-01-87 12:53p
     1 File(s)   1213440 bytes free

If you simply invoke DIR with a file name, like this:

[C:\] DIR FILENAME

the extension defaults to *.

Examples   In the following example, DIR will display
a directory listing of each of the files on drive B:

    [C:\] DIR B:

This command is functionally equivalent to

    [C:\] DIR B:*.*

or

    [C:\] B:
    [B:\] DIR

If several files exist on drive B, many may scroll off
the screen during the directory listing. If this happens,
invoke DIR with the /P qualifier, as shown here:

    [C:\] DIR B:*.* /P

Each time DIR completes a screenful of files, it will
pause, displaying the prompt

    Strike a key when ready. . .

When this occurs, simply press any key and DIR will
continue.

The file specification of the DIR command can be
quite specific, as shown here:

[C:\] DIR \DOS\CONFIG.OLD

This command will display the directory listing of the CONFIG.OLD file, which resides in the \ DOS sub-directory on the current disk.

If you are not interested in file sizes or date and time stamps, simply invoke DIR with the /W option:

[C:\] DIR /W

DIR will display a directory listing of file names only, five files across the screen, without the size, date, and time fields.

The DOS redirection operators can also be used with DIR. In this example, DOS will display a sorted directory listing:

[C:\] DIR | SORT

In a similar manner, this command prints the files in the current directory:

[C:\] DIR > PRN:

▶ **DISKCOMP**

Function   Compares two floppy disks.

Format

[*drive:*][*path*]DISKCOMP [*primary_drive:*
[*secondary_drive*]][/1] [/8]

where the following is true:

primary_drive specifies one of the floppy disk
drives to be used for the disk comparison. If you
do not specify a primary drive, DISKCOMP will
use the current default.

secondary_drive specifies the second drive to be
used for the disk comparison. If you do not
specify a secondary drive, DISKCOMP will use
the current default.

/1 directs DISKCOMP to perform a single-sided
disk comparison.

/8 directs DISKCOMP to perform an
eight-sector-per-track disk comparison.

Notes   If you have a single-floppy system, DISK-
COMP will perform a single-drive comparison,
prompting you to enter the source and target disks at
the correct time.

If the contents of the disks are identical, DISK-
COMP displays the message

Diskettes compare OK.

Otherwise, DISKCOMP displays the side and track (in hexadecimal) of the differences.

Examples   In the following example, DISKCOMP will compare the contents of the disk in drive A to that in drive B:

    [C:\] DISKCOMP A: B:

If the disks are identical, DISKCOMP will display

    Compare OK.

Otherwise, DISKCOMP will display the locations of the differences, as shown here:

    Compare error on
    side n track n

If you need to compare single-sided disks, use DISKCOMP as shown here:

    [C:\] DISKCOMP A: B: /1

▶ DISKCOPY

Function   Copies the contents of a source floppy disk to a target floppy disk.

Format

[drive:][path]DISKCOPY [source_drive:
[target_drive]][/1]

where the following is true:

source_drive specifies the disk drive that contains
the floppy disk to copy. If you do not specify a
source drive, DISKCOPY will use the current
default.

target_drive specifies the disk drive that contains
the disk to be copied to. If you do not specify a
target drive, DISKCOPY will use the current
default.

/1 directs DISKCOPY to copy only the first side
of the source disk to the target disk.

Notes DISKCOPY copies the contents of one floppy
disk to another. If you have a single-floppy system,
DISKCOPY will perform a single-drive copy, prompting you to enter the source and target disks at the correct time.

DISKCOPY does not correct disk fragmentation; instead, you should use the DOS XCOPY command for
that purpose.

DISKCOPY destroys the previous contents of the
target disk.

If the source and target disks are not the same type (a 360K and a 1.2MB disk, for example), DISKCOPY will display a message and terminate.

If the target disk has not yet been formatted, DISK-COPY will format the disk during the copy operation, displaying the message

Formatting while copying

Do not use DISKCOPY with JOINed or SUBSTed disks.

Examples The following command assumes that you have two compatible floppy disk drives on your system:

[C:\] DISKCOPY A: B:

Once DISKCOPY begins copying a disk, it will read several tracks of data from the source and then write them to the target disk. In a single floppy drive system, DISKCOPY repeats this process, prompting you for the source and target disks.

▶ ECHO

Function Displays or suppresses batch-command messages.

Format

ECHO [ON | OFF | *message*]

where the following is true:

ON enables the display of batch commands as they execute.

OFF disables the display of batch commands as they execute.

message contains the text that ECHO is to display to the user.

Notes   By default, each time you execute DOS batch files, DOS displays the name of each command as it executes. For example, the file

A
B
C

will display

[C:\]A

[C:\]B

[C:\]C

ECHO allows you to suppress the display of command names within a DOS batch file as the command executes. In this case, the file

```
ECHO OFF
A
B
C
```

will display

```
[C:\] ECHO OFF
```

ECHO also provides a convenient way to display messages for the end user.

If you invoke ECHO without a command-line parameter, ECHO will display its current state, ON or OFF.

Examples   In the following example, DOS will continue to display command names within a DOS batch file as it executes:

```
[C:\] ECHO ON
```

In a similar manner, this command disables command-name display:

```
[C:\] ECHO OFF
```

ECHO can be used with batch parameters as shown here:

```
ECHO %0
```

The following command displays the name of the batch file that is currently executing. This batch procedure displays each of its command-line parameters.

```
ECHO OFF
:LOOP
SHIFT
IF '%0'== '' GOTO DONE
ECHO %0
GOTO LOOP
:DONE
```

This ECHO command displays a simple message to the user:

```
ECHO This is a message via ECHO
```

As you can see, the following batch file fully exploits ECHO by displaying copyright information on the screen:

```
ECHO OFF
ECHO ********************************************
ECHO * Kevin Shafer Software, Inc. 1988    *
ECHO *                                      *
ECHO * Warriors Basketball -- 1988          *
ECHO *                                      *
ECHO ********************************************
```

▶ ERASE

Function   Erases a file from a disk.

Format

   ERASE [*drive:*][*path*] *file_name* [*.ext*]

where the following is true:

   file_name[*.ext*] is the name of the file to be
   deleted. ERASE fully supports DOS wild-card
   characters.

Notes   Unless overridden with a drive or path specifier,
ERASE will only delete files in the current directory.
If you attempt to erase all of the files in a directory, DOS
will first prompt you with

   Are you sure (Y/N)?

to ensure that you actually want the command performed. If you want to delete the files, press Y and press ENTER; otherwise, press N and press ENTER.

ERASE will not remove subdirectories. Use RMDIR for this purpose.

ERASE and DEL are functionally equivalent; most people use DEL.

Warning: Once you have erased a file, DOS cannot retrieve it.

Examples   In the following example, ERASE will erase the contents of the CONFIG.OLD file from drive B:

    [C:\] ERASE B:CONFIG.OLD

In a similar manner, the command

    [C:\] ERASE \DOS\COMMANDS\STARTUP.BAK

erases a file from within a DOS subdirectory.

If you attempt to delete all of the files in the current directory, like this:

    [C:\] ERASE *.*

ERASE will respond with

    Are you sure (Y/N)?

If you want to delete the files, press Y and press ENTER; otherwise, press N and press ENTER.

▶ EXIT

Function   Terminates the system's secondary command processor.

Format

    EXIT

Example   To terminate a secondary command processor, use the EXIT command like this:

    [C:\] EXIT

▶ FASTOPEN

Function   Increases the number of directory entries that DOS keeps in memory.

Format

    [*drive:*][*path*] FASTOPEN *d:* [*=entries*] [...]

where the following is true:

    d: specifies the disk drive for which DOS is setting aside storage space to contain directory entries.

entries specifies the number of directory entries for which DOS is reserving space. This value must be in the range 10-999; the default is 34.

... indicates that FASTOPEN can reserve space for several disks in one command.

Notes   FASTOPEN is a DOS 3.3 command. It increases the speed with which DOS locates files on disk.

Each time DOS accesses a directory, it will place that directory name into a list of the directory names. When you issue a directory manipulation command, DOS first checks its list of directories in memory to see if it can locate the directory on disk, instead of having to read the disk in search of the directory.

If several disks are specified, the sum of the entries cannot exceed 999. Each directory entry stored requires 35 bytes. If you use a value of 999 for directory entries, DOS will spend a considerable amount of overhead simply searching its directory list. Most users, therefore, find the default value of 34 acceptable.

Example   In the following example, DOS will remember 50 directory entries for drive C:

    [C:\] FASTOPEN C:=50

▶ FDISK

Function   Defines disk partitions on a DOS fixed disk.

Format

[*drive:*] [*path*] FDISK

Notes   DOS allows you to divide your fixed disk into logical collections of cylinders, called partitions. By so doing, you can actually place several different operating systems on one fixed disk. The DOS FDISK command allows you to add, change, display, and delete disk partitions.

The first sector on any fixed disk contains a master boot record, which contains information that defines which partition the computer uses for booting. FDISK is your means of interfacing with the master boot record.

▶ FIND

Function   Searches a file, several files, or piped input for a string.

Format

> [*drive:*][*path*] FIND [/C][/N][/V] "*string*" [*file_spec*]
> [...]

where is following is true:

/C directs FIND to display a count of occurrences of the string.

/N directs FIND to precede each line containing the string with its line number.

/V directs FIND to display each line that does not contain the string.

string specifies the string that FIND is to search for. It must be in quotes.

file_spec is the name of the file to be searched for the string. It can be a series of file names separated by spaces. FIND does not support DOS wild-card characters.

... indicates that several file names can reside in the command line.

Notes FIND allows you to quickly locate a sequence of characters within a file or within redirected output. FIND can also be used as a filter with piped input.

The string FIND is searching for must be in quotes. If the string has quotes nested within it, you must use two quotes for each nested quote, as in

[C:\] FIND """Look"" he said" FILENAME.EXT

If /C and /N are used together, FIND ignores /N.

Examples In the following example, FIND is used as a filter to list each subdirectory in the current directory:

[C:\] DIR A: | FIND "<DIR>"

To list all files that are not directories, use the FIND /V option, as shown here:

[C:\] DIR A: | FIND /V "<DIR>"

The following command displays each occurrence of the string *begin* in the TEST.PAS file:

[C:\] FIND "begin" TEST.PAS

In a similar manner, the following command displays each occurrence of *begin*. However, in this example, each line is preceded by its line number:

[C:\] FIND /N "begin" TEST.PAS

The following command simply displays the number of occurrences of *begin* in the file:

[C:\] FIND /C "begin" TEST.PAS

▶ FOR

Function   Provides repetitive execution (iterative processing) of DOS commands.

Format

FOR %%*variable* IN (*set*) DO *DOS_command*

where the following is true:

%%*variable* is the FOR loop control variable that DOS manipulates with each iteration. The variable name is restricted to a character; 0-9 cannot be used, since they are reserved for DOS batch parameters.

set is a list of valid DOS file names. This list can contain DOS file names separated by commas (A, B, C) wild-card characters (*,*), or both (A, B, *.DAT).

DOS_command is the command to be executed with each iteration.

Notes   FOR is used most commonly within DOS batch files. FOR can also be used from the DOS prompt. The %% symbols before the variable name are used in batch files; the single % symbol is used from the DOS prompt.

The set processing performed by FOR is quite straightforward. Consider this example:

FOR %%V IN (AUTOEXEC.BAT, CONFIG.SYS,
STARTUP.CMD) DO TYPE %%V

In this case, FOR will assign the variable the file name
AUTOEXEC.BAT during the first iteration and type its
contents. On the second iteration, FOR assigns the variable the file name CONFIG.SYS and displays its contents. On the third iteration, FOR assigns the variable
the file name STARTUP.CMD and again displays the
file's contents. When FOR prepares for the fourth iteration, it fails to find any more file names, so its processing is complete.

Examples   In the following example, the user has issued the command from the DOS prompt. Note that the
variable name is preceded by only one percent sign (%I)
when FOR is invoked from the DOS command line.

    [C:\] FOR %I IN (*.FOR) DO TYPE %I

In the following example, a DOS batch file is using
FOR to compile all of the C files on the current directory:

    FOR %%F IN (*.C) DO CC %%F

► FORMAT

Function   Formats a disk for use by DOS.

Format

> [*drive:*] [*path*] FORMAT [*d:*]
> [/S][/V][/4][/T:*tracks*] [/N:*sectors*][/1][/8][/B]

where the following is true:

d: is the name of the disk drive that contains the disk to be formatted.

/S directs FORMAT to place the DOS system files on the disk, making the disk bootable.

/V directs FORMAT to include the volume label.

/4 directs FORMAT to format the disk as double-sided in a quadruple-density disk drive.

/T:*tracks* defines the number of tracks to a side. This is a DOS 3.3 qualifier.

/N:*sectors* defines the numbers of sectors to a track. This is a DOS 3.3 qualifier.

/1 directs FORMAT to format the disk as a single-sided disk.

/8 directs FORMAT to format the disk with 8 sectors per track; most disks use 9 or 15 sectors.

/B directs FORMAT to reserve space for the system files on the target disk. Unlike the /S qualifier, /B does not actually place the files on disk.

Notes   When you purchase floppy disks, the original disk manufacturer has no way of knowing on what computer the disks will be used—or on what operating system. Therefore, before you can use a new disk, you must format it for DOS.

Warning: FORMAT destroys any of the information contained on the target disk.

Because inadvertently formatting a fixed disk can be disastrous, FORMAT will first prompt you with

```
WARNING, ALL DATA ON NON-REMOVABLE
DISK
DRIVE N: WILL BE LOST!
Proceed with Format (Y/N)?
```

before continuing. To proceed with the formatting process, press Y; otherwise, press N.

Upon completion, FORMAT will display the following:

- Total disk space

- Corrupted disk space marked as defective

- Total disk space consumed by the operating system

- Total disk space available for file utilization

As you can see, FORMAT reports on defective space that it finds during formatting. In addition, FOR-

MAT places entries for each defective sector into the file-allocation table, which prevents DOS from using the corrupted sectors for data storage.

The FORMAT /S command copies to the target disk the DOS hidden files that are required to boot DOS. FORMAT does not allow you to use /S and /V with the /B qualifier.

FORMAT will not work with drives that are in a network configuration.

Examples The following command makes the disk in drive B bootable:

[C:\] FORMAT B:/S

Many users often have to format double-density disks in their 1.2MB drives. The /4 qualifier in the FOR-MAT command directs FORMAT to create a 360K disk:

[C:\] FORMAT A:/4

Upon invocation, the command will display the following:

Insert a new diskette in drive A:
and press Enter when ready.

The /B and /S qualifiers are very similar. The following command directs FORMAT to reserve space for the operating system's boot files instead of placing those files on disk. If you include the /B qualifier, the DOS SYS command can later update the disk as required.

    [C:\] FORMAT A: /B

GOTO

Function   Branches to a label that is specified in a BAT file.

Format

    GOTO label_name

where the following is true:

    label_name specifies the name of a label within a
    DOS batch procedure.

Notes   DOS label names contain any of the characters valid for DOS file names. If the label does not exist, DOS terminates execution of the batch file.

DOS label names can be virtually any length. However, DOS only distinguishes the first eight characters of a label name. Hence, it will consider the label names DOS_LABEL1 and DOS_LABEL2 to be equivalent, since their first eight characters are equivalent.

label names DOS_LABEL1 and DOS_LABEL2 to be
equivalent, since their first eight characters are
equivalent.

Example   The following batch procedure displays a
continuous directory listing until the user presses CTRL-
C or CTRL-BREAK:

```
:LOOP
DIR
GOTO LOOP
```

Upon invocation, the procedure will repeatedly display
a directory listing of the current drive.

When DOS cannot find the label specified in a
GOTO command, it terminates the processing, as
shown here:

```
GOTO DOSLABEL
DATE
TIME
:DOSLABL
```

The procedure will display

```
Label not found
```

▶ GRAFTABL

Function   Allows the extended character set when the display is in graphics mode.

Format

[*drive:*][*path*]GRAFTABL [*code_page* | /STATUS]

where the following is true:

code_page specifies the code page to be used for the display. Possible values are as follows:

437	United States	863	French Canadian
850	Multilingual	865	Nordic
860	Portuguese		

/STATUS directs GRAFTABL to display the code page that is currently in use.

Notes   The DOS GRAFTABL command allows you to display extended ASCII characters when the display is in medium-resolution graphics mode.

GRAFTABL loads memory resident code when it is invoked, so it can only be invoked one time.

Examples   If you specify the /STA qualifier in the GRAFTABL command line, like this:

C> GRAFTABL /STATUS

GRAFTABL will display the number of the current code page, as shown here:

USA version of Graphic Character Set Table is already loaded.

The command

C> GRAFTABL 437

directs GRAFTABL to use the code page for the United States when it displays extended characters.

▶ GRAPHICS

Function   Allows screen contents containing graphics to be printed by means of print-screen operations.

Format

[*drive:*][*path*]GRAPHICS [*printer_type*][/B][/R]

where the following is true:

printer_type specifies the target printer type. Possible values are as follows:

COLOR1	Color printer with black ribbon
COLOR4	Color printer with RGB ribbon
COLOR8	Color printer with cyan, magenta, yellow, and black ribbon
COMPACT	Compact printer
GRAPHICS	Graphics printer

/B directs GRAPHICS to print the background color. The default is not to print the background color.

/R directs GRAPHICS to reverse the color of the screen image—black images on the screen will be printed as white, and white images as black.

Note   GRAPHICS is a memory resident program, so you should only install it once.

Example   The following command loads the memory resident software required to support print-screen operations that contain graphics images:

[C:\] GRAPHICS

▶ IF

Function   Provides conditional processing within DOS batch files.

Format

IF [NOT] *condition DOS_command*

where the following is true:

NOT performs a Boolean NOT on the result of *condition*.

condition must be one of the following:

- ERRORLEVEL *value* (True if program exit status >= value)

- EXIST *file_spec*   (True if the specified file exists)

- *string1*= =*string2* (True if both strings are identical)

DOS_command is the name of the command that DOS is to perform if *condition* is true.

Note   Although most users only utilize the DOS IF statement from within DOS batch files, DOS fully supports IF from the command line, as shown here:

[C:\] IF EXIST CONFIG.SYS TYPE CONFIG.SYS

Examples   In the following example, if the CONFIG.SYS file exists in the current directory, DOS will copy the file to drive B:

IF EXIST CONFIG.SYS COPY CONFIG.SYS B:

Here, if the DOSPGM program exits with a status greater than or equal to 3, DOS will display the message T H R E E:

```
ECHO OFF
DOSPGM
IF ERRORLEVEL 3 ECHO T H R E E
```

Note that you can simply add the Boolean NOT to the previous expression, which will direct the program to terminate if the exit status is less than 3:

```
ECHO OFF
DOSPGM
IF NOT ERRORLEVEL 3 GOTO DONE
ECHO T H R E E
:DONE
```

The following example uses the DOS IF command to determine whether or not the value of the batch parameter is NULL:

```
IF '%1' == " GOTO NULL
```

If you use this expression within the following batch file, you can echo each of the batch-file parameters to the screen:

```
ECHO OFF
:LOOP
SHIFT
IF '%0'== '' GOTO DONE
ECHO %0
GOTO LOOP
:DONE
```

If you invoke the procedure with

```
[C:\] ECHOTEST 1 2 3 4 5
```

it will display

```
[C:\] ECHOTEST 1 2 3 4 5
[C:\] ECHO OFF
1
2
3
4
5
```

▶ JOIN

Function   Joins a disk drive to a DOS path.

Format

[drive:][path]JOIN [d1: [d2:path]][/D]

where the following is true:

d1: specifies the disk drive to be joined to the path provided.

d2:path specifies the directory to be joined.

/D directs JOIN to disconnect a previously joined disk.

Notes   JOIN makes two disks appear as one by joining a disk to a DOS path.

If you issue a JOIN command without including any parameters, JOIN will display the current joins.

DOS will only join a disk to a DOS directory that is empty.

Do not use JOIN in conjunction with the BACKUP, CHKDSK, DISKCOMP, DISKCOPY, FDISK, FORMAT, LABEL, RECOVER, RESTORE, or SYS command.

Examples   Before you can join a disk to a directory, you must create an empty directory by using MKDIR:

[C:\] MKDIR \ JOINDIR

Next, use JOIN to connect a disk to the subdirectory, as shown here:

[C:\] JOIN B: \ JOINDIR

In this case, references to C:\ JOINDIR are identical to references to drive B. If drive B contains DOS subdirectories, simply refer to them as

[C:\] DIR \ JOINDIR\SUBDIR

Invoking JOIN without command-line parameters displays the current joins:

[C:\] JOIN

To remove a join, use the /D qualifier, as shown in this example:

[C:\] JOIN A: /D

▶ **KEYB**

Function   Loads a foreign keyboard set.

Format

[*drive:*][*path*] KEYB *xx* [*yy*]

where the following is true:

xx is the country code.

yy is the numeric code page.

Notes   In order to fully support international con-
figurations, DOS provides support for various
keyboard templates.

KEYB loads memory resident software to replace
the standard keyboard layout supported by ROM-
BIOS. Once a new keyboard is installed, you can tog-
gle between it and the default keyboard by pressing
CTRL-ALT-F1 for the default keyboard and CTRL-ALT-F2
for the foreign keyboard. Common keyboard layouts
include

KEYB FR	France
KEYB GR	Germany
KEYB IT	Italy
KEYB SP	Spain
KEYB UK	United Kingdom
KEYB US	United States

Example   In the following example, DOS will use the
United Kingdom keyboard template:

C> KEYB UK

▶ LABEL

Function   Specifies a disk volume label.

Format

[*drive:*] [*path*] LABEL [*target_drive:*]
[*volume_label*]

where the following is true:

target_drive: is the disk drive that contains the disk to be labeled.

volume_label is the 11-character volume label desired. All characters that are valid in DOS file names are valid volume label characters.

Notes   DOS allows you to define a name for each of your disks. Each time you issue the DIR command, it displays the volume label of the disk for which it is displaying the directory, as shown here:

```
Volume in drive A is DOSLABEL
Directory of  A:\
```

It is also possible to use software to obtain the disk volume label from within your DOS programs. By so doing, you can ensure that the user has the correct disk in each drive.

If you do not specify a volume label in the command line, LABEL will prompt you for one:

```
Volume in drive C is DOSDISK
Volume label (11 characters, ENTER for none)?
```

If you do not want to change the disk label, simply press ENTER; otherwise, type in the volume name desired.

The DOS VOL command also displays the disk volume label (see VOL).

Example   The following command gives the name DOSDISK to the floppy disk contained in drive B. Since the command line contains the desired label name, LABEL did not have to prompt the user for any information:

   [C:\] LABEL B:DOSDISK

In this command however, the label name is not specified in the command line:

   [C:\] LABEL

In such a case, LABEL will prompt

   Volume in drive C is DOSDISK
   Volume label (11 characters, ENTER for none)?

Either type in the volume label that you desire or press the ENTER key to leave the current label name unchanged.

▶ MKDIR

Function   Creates a DOS subdirectory.

Format

   MKDIR [*drive:*] *path*

or

MD [*drive:*] *path*

where the following is true:

drive: specifies the drive on which to create the subdirectory. If a drive is not specified, MKDIR will use the current default.

path specifies the name of the DOS directory that MKDIR is to create.

Notes   Every DOS directory has a root directory (\) from within which all other subdirectories grow. If you do not use DOS subdirectories, your disks are restricted to a limited number of files.

Each time you create a DOS subdirectory, MKDIR has two choices. First, if the directory name starts with a slash, as in \ SUBDIR, DOS will start with the root directory to create the subdirectory. If, however, the name does not start with a slash, as in SUBDIR, DOS will create the directory within the current directory.

Use the following rules of thumb when you create your DOS directories:

• DOS directory names conform to the same format as DOS file names, with an eight-character file name followed by an optional three-character extension. The following are examples of valid DOS directory names: FILENAME.EXT, HARDWARE.SAL, and SOFTWARE.INV.

- The maximum path name that DOS can process is 63 characters.

- If you do not specify a complete DOS path name when you create a subdirectory, DOS assumes that you are creating the directory in the current directory.

- To manipulate directories contained on other disks, simply precede the directory name with a disk-drive identifier such as B:\FINANCE\CAR.

- Do not create directory names that are identical to the names of files contained in the same directory.

- Do not create a directory called \DEV. DOS uses a hidden directory called \DEV to communicate with hardware devices.

- Root directories on each disk are restricted to a specific number of files because of the disk layout. Subdirectories, however, can contain an unlimited number of files.

- Divide your disk logically into subdirectories.

Examples   In the following example, MKDIR will create a directory called IBM in the root:

```
[C:\] MKDIR \IBM
```

In a similar manner, the command

```
[C:\] MKDIR \IBM\NOTES
```

creates a subdirectory called NOTES in the IBM directory. This command is equivalent to the commands

```
[C:\] CHDIR \IBM
[C:\] MKDIR NOTES
```

Note that the second command does not have a slash in front of the directory name NOTES. If it did, MKDIR would create the directory in the root instead of in the \IBM subdirectory.

Assuming that the current directory is still the root, the command

```
[C:\] MKDIR MISC
```

also creates a subdirectory off of the root. In this case, the subdirectory name does not contain a slash, so MKDIR creates the directory in the current directory, which in this case is still the root. Had the current directory been other than the root, the correct command would have been

```
[C:\] MKDIR \MISC
```

▶ MODE

Function   Specifies device characteristics.

Format

[*drive:*] [*path*] MODE *n*

or

[*drive:*] [*path*] MODE [*n*],*m*, [T]

or

[*drive:*] [*path*] MODE COM#[:] *baud* [,*parity*
[,*data* [,*stop* [, P]]]]

or

[*drive:*] [*path*] MODE LPT#[:] [*cpl*] [,*vli*] [, P]

or

[*drive:*] [*path*] MODE LPT#[:] =COM#[:]

where the following is true:

baud specifies the device baud rate (110, 150,
300, 600, 1200, 2400, 4800, 9600, or 19200).
MODE only requires you to specify the first two
digits of the baud rate.

n specifies the screen display attribute. It must be one of the following:

40	Specifies 40-column display
80	Specifies 80-column display
BW40	Specifies a black-and-white 40-column display
BW80	Specifies a black-and-white 80-column display
CO40	Specifies a color 40-column display
CO80	Specifies a color 80-column display
MONO	Specifies a monochrome display.

m specifies the direction in which the screen display will be shifted, either one character to the left or right.

T requests MODE to display a test pattern to aid in character alignment.

parity specifies the device parity (E for even parity, N for no parity, or O for odd parity). The default is even parity.

data specifies the number of data bits (7 or 8). The default is 7 data bits.

stop specifies the number of stop bits (1 or 2). For 110 baud, the default is 2; otherwise, it is 1.

cpl is characters per line (80, 132).

vli is vertical lines per inch (6, 8).

P specifies continuous retries on time-out errors.

LPT# specifies the parallel printer number, as in LPT1.

COM# specifies the serial port number, as in COM1.

Notes   Many hardware devices require unique data communication setups (for example, 4800 baud with even parity). The DOS MODE command allows you to set the characteristics of a port on the PC.

By default, DOS uses the parallel printer port for printed data. If your printer is connected to a serial device, you can redirect the parallel output to the serial device by using MODE.

If a device requires modification each time it is used, place the MODE command in AUTOEXEC.BAT.

Examples   The following command sets the screen display to 40 columns per line:

[C:\] MODE 40

Similarly, the command

[C:\] MODE 80

resets the screen to 80-column mode.

If you have a serial printer connected to your system, you must use MODE to route the printer data to the serial printer:

[C:\] MODE LPT1:=COM1:

This routes the parallel data from LPT1 to the serial port COM1.

The following command specifies the data communication parameters for COM1:

[C:\] MODE COM1 96,N,8,1

► MORE

Function   Displays a command's output a screenful at a time.

Format

DOS_command | [drive:] [path] MORE

or

[drive:] [path] MORE < DOS_command

where the following is true:

DOS_command is a DOS command.

Notes   The DOS MORE command reads data from the standard input device, displaying the information on the standard output device a page at a time until an end-of-file marker is encountered. Each time a page of data is displayed on the screen, MORE displays the message

-- MORE --

Simply press any key to continue the output, or press CTRL-C to terminate the command.

Examples   In the following example, MORE is used as a filter, obtaining its input from the standard input device (stdin):

[C:\] SORT < DATA.DAT | MORE

To display the contents of DATA.DAT one screenful at a time, use MORE as shown here:

[C:\] MORE < DATA.DAT

▶ **NLSFUNC**

Function   Provides device support for international code pages.

Format

[*drive:*][*path*]NLSFUNC [*file_spec*]

where the following is true:

file_spec is the complete DOS file specification
for the file that contains the country information.
This file is usually COUNTRY.SYS.

Notes   The NLSFUNC command works in conjunction with CHCP. You must invoke NLSFUNC before
you invoke CHCP.
This is a DOS 3.3 command.

Example   The following command informs DOS that
the country information file (COUNTRY.SYS) resides
in the \ SYSFILES directory on drive C:

    [C:\] NLSFUNC C:\SYSFILES\COUNTRY.SYS

▶ PATH

Function   Defines the search path for the command
files that DOS uses each time it fails to locate a command internally, within the current directory, or within
a specified directory.

Format

    PATH [*drive:*][*path* [;[*drive:*][*path*]...]

where the following is true:

drive: specifies the disk drive that DOS is to
include in the command-file search path.

path specifies a DOS subdirectory to be included in the command-file search path.

... indicates that a disk drive and subdirectory may be specified several times.

Notes   When DOS cannot find a command internally or in an EXE, COM, or BAT file in the current directory, it searches to see if the user has defined a command-file search path. The DOS PATH command allows you to define disk drives and subdirectories to be included in this search path.

Examples   In the following example, if DOS cannot find the command, it will search the root directories on drives C, B, and A, in that order:

   [C:\] PATH C:\;B:\;A:\

In a similar manner, the following PATH command directs DOS to search \DOS, \UTIL, and then \MISC:

   [C:\] PATH \DOS;\UTIL;\MISC

▶   **PAUSE**

Function   Displays an optional message, pausing batch-file execution.

Format

PAUSE [*message*]

where the following is true:

message is an optional message that PAUSE is to display each time it suspends batch processing. It can contain up to 123 characters.

Notes   When DOS encounters PAUSE within a batch file, it displays the following:

[optional message text]
Strike a key when ready . . .

To continue batch processing, press any key; otherwise, press CTRL-BREAK. If you press CTRL-BREAK, DOS will display

Terminate batch job (Y/N)?

To terminate the batch file, press Y; otherwise press N.
    The DOS ECHO OFF command suppresses the display of messages from PAUSE.

Examples   When DOS encounters the PAUSE command with a batch procedure, as shown here:

PAUSE Enter a blank disk in drive B

it will pause and display

    [C:\] PAUSE Enter a blank disk in drive B
    Strike a key when ready . . .

In a similar manner, the command

    PAUSE

will display

    [C:\] PAUSE
    Strike a key when ready . . .

▶ PRINT

Function   Prints a DOS file by means of the print
queue.

Format

    [drive:] [path] PRINT [/D:device_name] [/ C]
    [/T] [/B:buffer_size] [/M:max_ticks]
    [/Q:queue_size] [/S:time_slice] [/U:busy_ticks]
    fle_spec [...]

where the following is true:

    /D:device_name specifies the name of the device
    that DOS is to use for the printer. The default
    device is PRN.

/C directs PRINT to cancel the print job of the file whose name precedes the /C and all of those that follow.

/T directs PRINT to cancel all of the print jobs in the printer queue.

/B:*buffer_size* specifies the amount of memory (in bytes) that is set aside for PRINT. The default size is 512. By increasing this size in multiples of 512 (1024, 2048, 4096) you will improve PRINT's performance by decreasing the number of disk I/O operations required. Increasing this value does, however, consume memory.

/M:*max_ticks* specifies the maximum number of CPU clock ticks that PRINT can consume before it must return control to DOS. This value can be in the range from 1 to 255; the default value is 2. This qualifier is only valid the first time that you invoke PRINT. Increasing this value will improve PRINT's performance, since it has more control of the CPU. However, if you make this value too large, the rest of your applications will become sluggish when PRINT is working.

/Q:*queue_size* specifies the number of entries that the PRINT queue can store. This value must be in the range from 1 to 32; the default value is 10. This qualifier is only valid the first time you invoke PRINT.

/S:*time_slice* specifies the PRINT time slice. This value must be in the range from 1 to 255; the default value is 8. This qualifier is only valid the first time you invoke PRINT.

/U:*busy_ticks* specifies the number of CPU clock ticks that PRINT will wait in order for the printer to become available for the next series of characters. This value must be in the range from 1 to 255; the default value is 1. This qualifier is only valid the first time you invoke PRINT.

file_spec is the complete DOS path name of the file to be added to or removed from the print queue. PRINT supports DOS wild-card characters.

...indicates that several file names can be placed on the PRINT command line.

Notes   PRINT sends files to the printer in background mode, allowing you to continue your processing in the foreground.

CPU clock ticks occur 18.2 times per second on the IBM PC.

Examples   The following command installs a print queue with storage for 32 files:

    [C:\] PRINT /Q:32

Remember that many qualifiers are only valid the first time you issue a PRINT command.

This command prints all of the files in the current directory that have an extension of DAT:

[C:\] PRINT *.DAT

In a similar manner, this command simply prints the CONFIG.SYS file:

[C:\] PRINT CONFIG.SYS

The following command terminates all current print jobs:

[C:\] PRINT /T

This command removes the STARTUP.CMD file from the print queue:

[C:\] PRINT STARTUP.CMD /C

▶ PROMPT

Function   Defines the DOS prompt that appears on your screen display.

Format

PROMPT [*prompt_string*]

where the following is true:

prompt_string is the character string that defines the DOS prompt. It can contain characters or the following metastrings:

$b	I character	$p	Current directory
$d	Date	$q	= character
$e	ESC	$t	Current time
$h	Backspace	$v	DOS version
$g	> character	$	CR LF
$l	< character	$$	$ character

Note   If no string is specified, PROMPT resets the system prompt to the current default drive.

Examples   The following command simply sets the users prompt to YES:

```
[C:\] PROMPT YES$g
YES>
```

This command sets the system prompt to the current system time:

```
[C:\] PROMPT $t

15:20:18.81
15:20:43.78
15:20:87.12
```

The DOS prompt can be used to keep track of the current directory. In this case, the command

[C:\] PROMPT [$p]

directs DOS to display the current directory name as the system prompt:

[C:\SUBDIR]

▶ **RECOVER**

Function   Recovers a damaged disk or file.

Format

[*drive:*][*path*]RECOVER [*d:*][*p*]*file_name.ext*

where the following is true:

d: is the disk-drive identifier of the file or disk to be recovered. If you do not specify this parameter, RECOVER will use the current default.

p is the DOS path name of the subdirectory that contains the file to be recovered. If you do not specify this parameter, DOS will use the current default.

file_name.ext is the name of the damaged file to be recovered.

Notes   If a DOS disk or file becomes damaged and loses sectors, you can use the DOS RECOVER command to retrieve portions of the disk or file up to the point of the corruption.

If the file is a text file, you can edit the file later and restore the missing contents. If, however, the file is an executable file, you should not execute it—remember, the file is missing sectors. Instead, maintain a good backup of your files so that you do not have to rely on RECOVER.

If you use RECOVER to recover a complete disk, RECOVER will create files in the root directory with names in the form FILE*nnnn*.REC, where *nnnn* represents a four-digit number that begins with 0001 (FILE0001.REC).

RECOVER does not work with disk drives connected to a network.

Examples   The following command attempts to recover the contents of the disk in drive A:

    [C:\] RECOVER A:

In this case, RECOVER will create several files whose name are in the format FILE*nnnn*.REC. The command

    [C:\] RECOVER FILENAME.EXT

will recover the contents of the FILENAME.EXT file up to the damaged sector.

▶ REM

Function   Displays comments during the execution of batch files.

Format

REM [*message*]

where the following is true:

message is a character string of up to 123 characters.

Notes   REM allows you to display messages through the standard output device during the execution of batch (BAT) files. An optional command-line parameter can contain the message. The DOS ECHO OFF command inhibits the display of messages by REM.

Example   The following shows the use of REM in a batch file:

```
:LOOP
REM About to display the directory listing
DIR
REM Directory listing complete
REM
GOTO LOOP
```

▶ RENAME

Function   Renames the specified file or files.

Format

   REN *file_spec file_name* [*.ext*]

or

   RENAME *file_spec file_name* [*.ext*]

where the following is true:

   file_spec is the complete DOS path name of the
   file to be renamed. It can contain a drive and DOS
   subdirectory path. RENAME supports DOS
   wild-card characters for this parameter.

   file_name is the target file name for the rename
   operation. It cannot have a drive or DOS
   subdirectory path. RENAME supports DOS
   wild-card characters for this parameter.

.*ext* is an optional extension for the target file
name.

Notes   The target file must reside in the same directory
on the same disk drive as the source file. This is because
RENAME does not copy a file's contents, but simply
renames the file in its directory entry.

Examples   The following command gives all of the
files on drive B that have the extension BAK the same
file name with a new extension of SAV:

   [C:\] REN B:*.BAK *.SAV

In a similar manner, the command

   [C:\] RENAME \DOS*.SYS *.XXX

changes the extension of all SYS files in the \DOS
directory to XXX.

   The target file must reside in the same disk and directory as the source, so if you specify a disk-drive identifier for the target file, REN will display the following:

   Invalid parameter

▶ **REPLACE**

Function   Allows selective file replacements and updates when new versions of software become available.

Format

[*drive:*][*path*]REPLACE *source_file_spec*
[*target_file_spec*][/A][/P][/R][/S][/W]

where the following is true:

source_file_spec is the complete DOS file specification for the files that REPLACE is to use in the file replacement. REPLACE supports DOS wild-card characters.

target_file_spec is the complete DOS file specification of the destination of the files being added or released.

/A directs REPLACE to add files to the target directory instead of replacing them. With this qualifier, REPLACE only places those files onto the target that are not currently present.

/P directs REPLACE to prompt you with

Do you want to replace drive:filename.ext (Y/N)?

before adding or replacing files.

/R directs REPLACE to also replace the files on the target location that are currently marked as read-only. Without this qualifier, REPLACE stops replacement operations with the first file marked read-only.

/S directs REPLACE to search the subdirectories on the target location for other occurrences of the file to be replaced. This qualifier cannot be used with /A.

/W directs REPLACE to prompt

Press any key to begin replacing file(s).

before starting the file-replacement operations.

Note   REPLACE is a convenient utility for software developers, allowing them to easily select specific files for replacement.

Examples   The following command will replace any files in the root directory on drive A that have the extension A:

   [C:\] REPLACE *.A A:\

In the same manner, the command

   [C:\] REPLACE *.A A:\A

will replace all of the files in the \A subdirectory on drive A that have the extension A. The command

   [C:\] REPLACE *.* A:\ /S

updates all of the files on the entire disk in drive A (even those in subdirectories) that are found on the source disk. As you can see, REPLACE makes your file updates very straightforward.

▶ RESTORE

Function   Restores files saved previously by the BACKUP command.

Format

[*drive:*] [*path*] RESTORE *source_drive:file_spec*
target_drive:file_spec [/ P] [/S] [/B:*mm-dd-yy*]
[/A:*mm-dd-yy*] [/ E:*hh:mm:ss*] [/ L:*hh:mm:ss*]
[/ M] [/ N]

where the following is true:

source_drive:file_spec specifies the files to be restored. Each file name must match the name of the file as it was originally backed up;
source_drive is the drive that contains the backup files.

target_drive:file_spec is the disk drive to which the files will be restored.

/P directs RESTORE to prompt to the user before restoring those files that have been modified or set to read-only since the backup.

/S directs RESTORE to restore files contained in subdirectories.

/B:*mm-dd-yy* directs RESTORE to restore only those files modified on or before the specified date.

/A:*mm-dd-yy* directs RESTORE to restore only those files modified after the specified date.

/E:*hh:mm:ss* directs RESTORE to restore only those files modified at or before the time specified. This is a DOS 3.3 qualifier.

/L:*hh:mm:ss* directs RESTORE to restore only those files modified at or before the time specified. This is a DOS 3.3 qualifier.

/M directs RESTORE to restore only those files modified since the last backup.

/N directs RESTORE to restore only those files no longer existing on the target disk.

Notes   The DOS BACKUP command places files onto a disk in a manner only accessible by RESTORE. To copy a file from the backup disk, you must use RESTORE. RESTORE will not restore hidden system files or the DOS COMMAND.COM command processor.

Examples   The following command restores all files from the backup disk in drive A, including those in subdirectories:

[C:\] RESTORE A: C:*.* /S

If the backup uses several floppy disks, RESTORE will prompt you to place subsequent disks in the specified drive each time it needs a new backup disk.

This command restores all of the files from the backup disk that contain the extension DAT:

[C:\] RESTORE A: C:*.DAT /P

RESTORE will prompt you with

Warning! File FILENAME.EXT was changed after backed up.
Replace the file (Y/N)?

before it restores files that have modified since the backup.

▶ RMDIR

Function Removes the specified directory.

Format

RMDIR [*drive:*] *path*

or

RD [*drive:*] *path*

where the following is true:

drive: specifies the drive from which the subdirectory will be removed. If this parameter is not specified, RMDIR will use the current default.

path specifies the name of the DOS subdirectory to remove.

Notes　RMDIR will only remove empty subdirectories that do not contain files.

The maximum path name that DOS can process is 63 characters.

Examples　The following command attempts to remove the IBM subdirectory from the root directory of the current drive. If the directory contains files, RMDIR cannot remove the directory.

　[C:\] RMDIR \IBM

Similarly, the command

　[C:\] RMDIR MISC\IBM\SALES

removes the subdirectory \ SALES from the directory \ MISC \ IBM on the current drive.

▶ SELECT

Function   Selects an international format for a new disk.

Format

> [*drive:*] [*path*] SELECT [[A: | B:] *d:* [*p*]]
> *country keyboard*

where the following is true:

A: | B: specifies the source drive of the keyboard files.

d: is the target drive to which international files are to be copied.

p is the target path for the file copy.

country is the three-digit code that specifies the country to be used.

keyboard is the two-character identifier that specifies the keyboard layout to be used.

Notes   SELECT uses the DISKCOPY command to make a copy of the DOS disk (DOS 3.2 uses XCOPY). It also creates CONFIG.SYS and AUTOEXEC.BAT, files that are required for international support on the target disk.

The following codes are supported:

FRANCE	033	KEYBFR.COM
GERMANY	049	KEYBGR.COM
ITALY	039	KEYBIT.COM
SPAIN	034	KEYBSP.COM
U.K.	044	KEYBUK.COM

Upon completion, SELECT will place the line

    COUNTRY=xxx

in CONFIG.SYS and

    KEYB XX

in AUTOEXEC.BAT on the target disk.

SELECT supports one or two floppy drive systems.

Example   The following command directs SELECT to create a disk that fully supports German language characteristics:

    [C:\] SELECT A: 049 GR

▶ **SET**

Function   Places or displays DOS environment entries.

Format

    SET [name=[value]]

108

where the following is true:

name is the name of the DOS environment entry to which you are assigning a value.

value is a character string that defines the assigned value.

Notes   When DOS boots, it reserves an area of memory called the environment, which provides a storage location for system specifics. DOS commands such as PROMPT and PATH place entries in the environment. The DOS SET command sets or displays entries in the DOS environment.

SET converts all entry names to uppercase.

SET with no parameters displays the current environment.

Examples   With no command-line parameters, SET displays the current environment entries:

```
[C:\] SET
COMSPEC=C:\COMMAND.COM
PATH=C:\DOS
```

In the following example, SET will create a new environment entry called FILE and assign it the value TEST.DAT:

```
[C:\] SET FILE=TEST.DAT
```

You can verify this by again issuing the SET command, as shown here:

```
[C:\] SET
COMSPEC=C:\COMMAND.COM
PATH=C:\DOS
FILE=TEST.DAT
```

To remove the value for an entry, use SET as shown here:

```
[C:\] SET FILE=
```

► SHARE

Function   Supports DOS file sharing.

Format

[*drive:*][*path*]SHARE [/F:*file_space*][/L:*locks*]

where the following is true:

/F:*file_space* allocates memory (in bytes) for the area in which DOS will store file-sharing information. Each open file requires 11 bytes plus the length of the file name (up to 63 characters). The default file space is 2048 bytes.

/L:*locks* allocates memory for the number of file locks desired. The default is 20.

Notes DOS versions 3.0 and greater support file and record locking. Each time a file is opened with file sharing installed, DOS checks to see if the file is locked against the open operation. If it is, the file cannot be opened. In addition, DOS checks for locking during each read and write operation.

SHARE is a memory-resident software program that performs the file and record locking; as such, it can only be installed once. Once it has been installed, the only way to remove file sharing is to reboot. SHARE places considerable overhead on all of your file operations, so you should only install it when file sharing is in effect.

Examples The following command invokes file sharing with default values of 2048 and 20 locks:

    [C:\] SHARE

This command installs file-sharing support with 40 locks:

    [C:\] SHARE /L:40

▶ SHIFT

Function Shifts each batch parameter one position to the left.

Format

    SHIFT

Notes   If more than ten parameters are passed to a DOS batch procedure, you can use the SHIFT command to access each parameter past %9. If no parameter exists to the right of a parameter, SHIFT will assign the parameter a NULL string.

Example   The following batch file displays all of the batch parameters specified on the command line:

```
ECHO OFF
:LOOP
SHIFT
IF '%0'== '' GOTO DONE
ECHO %0
GOTO LOOP
:DONE
```

If the previous file was named TEST.BAT, invoking the batch file as

    [C:\] TEST 1 2 3 4

would display

[C:\] ECHO OFF
1
2
3
4

▶ **SORT**

Function   Activates the DOS SORT filter.

Format

   DOS_command | [*drive:*] [*path*] SORT [/R]
   [/+*n*]

or

   [*drive:*][*path*]SORT [/R][/+*n*] *file*

where the following is true:

   DOS_command is a DOS command.

   /R directs SORT to sort the data in reverse order.

   /+*n* allows you to specify the column on which to
   sort the data.

Notes   The DOS SORT command reads data from the
   standard input device, sorting the information and displaying it on the standard output device until an end-
   of-file marker is encountered.

SORT is usually used as a filter with the DOS < and I redirection operators.

Examples   The following command directs SORT to sort the information contained in the DATA.DAT file:

[C:\] SORT < DATA.DAT

In a similar manner, the command

[C:\] SORT /R < DATA.DAT

directs SORT to sort the same file, this time in reverse order. Likewise, the command

[C:\] SORT /+6 < FILENAME.EXT

directs SORT to sort the file based on the data starting in column 6.

▶ SUBST

Function   Substitutes a drive name for a DOS path name.

Format

[*drive:*][*path*]SUBST [*d:*] [*path_name*][/D]

where the following is true:

d: is the disk-drive identifier that will be used to reference the path.

path_name is the DOS path name to be abbreviated.

/D directs SUBST to remove a previous disk substitution.

Notes   Because DOS path names can become quite long, DOS allows you to substitute a drive identifier for a path name.

If you invoke SUBST without any parameters, current substitutions will be displayed.

Examples   In the following example, DOS allows you to abbreviate the subdirectory \DOS\HELPFILE-\COMMANDS to the drive letter E:

    [C:\] SUBST E: \DOS\HELPFILE\COMMANDS

A command like

    [C:\] DIR E:

will then display the \DOS\HELPFILE\COMMANDS directory's contents. If that subdirectory contains other subdirectories, you can still use the drive letter, as shown here:

    [C:\] DIR E:SUBDIR

Invoking SUBST without including command-line parameters displays current substitutions:

```
[C:\] SUBST
E: => C:\DOS\HELPFILE\COMMANDS
```

▶ **SYS**

Function   Transfers to the target disk the hidden operating system files that perform the initial system startup.

Format

   [*drive:*][*path*]SYS *target_drive:*

where the following is true:

   target_drive: specifies the target disk drive for the hidden operating system files.

Notes   SYS does not copy the COMMAND.COM file to the target disk. To do so, you must use the DOS COPY command.

   DOS will only transfer files to an empty target disk or to a disk that was formatted previously with the /S or /B qualifier.

   SYS does not work with a JOINed or SUBSTed disk.

Example   In this example, SYS will transfer the hidden operating system files to the disk in drive A:

[C:\] SYS A:

Verify this by issuing the CHKDSK command, as shown here:

[C:\] CHKDSK A:

If the target disk cannot store the required system files, SYS will display

No room for system on destination disk

▶ TIME

Function   Sets the DOS system time.

Format

TIME [*HH:MM* [:*SS* [.*hh*]]]

where the following is true:

HH:MM is the desired hours (0-23) and minutes (0-59).

SS is the desired seconds (0-59).

hh is the desired hundredths of a second (0-99).

Notes   In the past, most DOS users had to use the Setup disk provided in the *Guide to Operations* manual to set the system clock. The DOS 3.3 TIME command

117

modifies the AT system clock, removing this requirement.

If you do not specify a time, TIME displays the current time.

Examples   If you do not specify a time on the command line:

    [C:\] TIME

TIME will prompt you for one, as shown here:

    Current time is 16:08:41.15
    Enter new time:

To leave the time unchanged, simply press ENTER. Otherwise, type in the time desired.

The following command sets the clock to 12:00 noon:

    [C:\] TIME 12:00

This command sets the clock to midnight:

    [C:\] TIME 00:00:00.000

If the time that you specify is invalid, as in

    [C:\] TIME 15:65:00

TIME will display an error message and reprompt you for the time, as shown here:

    Invalid time
    Enter new time:

▶ **TREE**

Function   Displays a directory structure.

Format

    [*drive:*] [*path*] TREE [*d:*] [/F]

where the following is true:

    d: is the disk-drive identifier of the disk for which TREE is to display the directory structure.

    /F directs TREE to display the name of each file in a directory as well.

Notes   By default, TREE displays the name of each directory on a disk. To also display each file name, use the /F qualifer.

Examples   The following command displays the directory structure of the disk:

    [C:\] TREE

To also display the files in each directory, use /F as shown here:

[C:\] TREE B:/F

▶ **TYPE**

Function   Displays a text file's contents.

Format

TYPE *file_spec*

where the following is true:

file_spec is the complete DOS file specification for the file to be displayed. It can contain a disk-drive identifier and DOS path name.

Notes   TYPE is restricted to ASCII files. Do not use TYPE with COM or EXE files—they contain characters that will cause your screen to beep and display uncommon characters.

Examples   The following command directs TYPE to display the contents of the CONFIG.SYS file:

[C:\] TYPE CONFIG.SYS

In a similar manner, the command

[C:\] TYPE B:\DOS\AUTOEXEC.SAV

directs TYPE to display the contents of the AUTO-EXEC.SAV file in the \DOS subdirectory on drive B.

If the file specified in the TYPE command line does not exist, TYPE will display

Invalid filename or file not found

 VER

Function Displays the DOS version number.

Format

VER

Note DOS version numbers are comprised of a major and minor version number. For example, DOS 3.2 has a major version number of 3 and a minor version number of 2.

Example The following command directs VER to display the current version number:

[C:\] VER

For DOS Version 3.3, the output is

IBM Personal Computer DOS Version 3.30

► VERIFY

Function   Enables or disables disk verification.

Format

VERIFY [ON | OFF]

where the following is true:

ON enables DOS disk verification.

OFF disables DOS disk verification.

Notes   Periodically, a disk drive may not correctly record the information on disk as DOS intended. Although this is very rare, such occurrences can leave incorrect data on your disk. If you enable disk I/O verification, DOS will double-check the data it writes to disk by rereading each sector and comparing it to the original data. If a discrepancy exists, DOS will detect it. However, because DOS must reread each sector that it writes to disk, disk verification causes significant system overhead.

Examples   The following command enables disk I/O verification:

[C:\] VERIFY ON

Invoking VERIFY without command-line parameters causes VERIFY to display its current state:

```
[C:\] VERIFY
VERIFY is on.

[C:\]
```

▶ VOL

Function   Displays a disk volume label.

Format

VOL [*drive:*]

where the following is true:

drive: specifies the disk drive that contains the disk for which VOL is to display the disk volume label. If you do not specify this parameter, VOL will use the current default.

Notes   DOS volume labels are 11-character names assigned to a disk. These labels can consist of the same characters as DOS file names.

To assign a volume label, you should use the DOS LABEL command.

Example   In the following example, VOL will display the disk volume label of the disk contained in the current drive:

    [C:\] VOL
    Volume in drive C is DOSDISK

▶ **XCOPY**

Function   Copies source files and subdirectories to a target destination.

Format

    [drive:] [path] XCOPY source_file_spec
    [target_file_spec] [/A] [/D:mm-dd-yy] [/E]
    [/M] [/P] [/V] [/S] [/W]

where the following is true:

source_file_spec is the complete DOS file specification for the source files to be copied by XCOPY.

target_file_spec is the destination name for the files copied by XCOPY.

/A directs XCOPY to copy only files that have the archive bit set.

/D:mm-dd-yy directs XCOPY to copy only those files created since the specified date.

/E directs XCOPY to place subdirectories on the target disk if the subdirectory is currently empty.

/M functions like the /A qualifier; however, /M directs XCOPY to clear each file's archive bit as it copies the file.

/P directs XCOPY to prompt

FILENAME.EXT (Y/N)?

before copying each file.

/V directs XCOPY to compare the contents of the target file and the source file to verify that the file copy was successful.

/S directs XCOPY to copy the contents of lower-level subdirectories to the target location.

/W directs XCOPY to prompt

Press any key to begin copying file(s)

before beginning.

Notes   XCOPY does more than COPY and DISK-COPY, in that it copies files contained in DOS sub-directories on a selective basis. Many users invoke XCOPY to repair disk fragmentation or use it as a system backup mechanism.

Examples   If you have a blank disk in drive B, the command

    [C:\] XCOPY A:*.* B:\ /S

will create a disk structure on the disk in drive B that is identical to the structure of the disk in drive A.

The following command will copy all of the files contained in or below the subdirectory \A on drive A to the disk in drive B:

    [C:\] XCOPY A:\A*.* B:\ /S

To use XCOPY to copy the entire contents of a fixed disk to floppy disks, first set the attribute of each file on the fixed disk to indicate that each requires a backup, as shown here:

    [C:\] ATTRIB +A *.* /S

Next, issue the command

    [C:\] XCOPY *.* A:\ /M /E /S

XCOPY will begin transferring files to the floppy disk, maintaining the existing disk structure. When the target disk becomes full, simply insert a new floppy disk in drive A and again invoke the command:

    [C:\] XCOPY *.* A:\ /M /E /S

XCOPY will continue where it left off, since it has been clearing the archive bit on each file it successfully copies to the target disk.

WHERE TO LOOK NEXT

If you have already read the Osborne/McGraw-Hill texts *DOS: The Complete Reference* and *DOS Power User's Guide,* you should strongly consider the DOS User's Group, which is the only international DOS user's group. Its members consist of novices, programmers, authors, MIS managers, secretaries, and many more. Annual membership is $25.00, which includes a quarterly newsletter on DOS topics, tutorials, and reviews. Write to

DOS User's Group
P.O. Box 26601
Las Vegas, NV 89126

This user's group offers you the latest DOS information. Don't hesitate to join.